ELLA
Diaries

TOP
SECRET!

Meredith Costain

Thanks to Inez, Isobel, Lila, Mia, Samilla and Tia for all their fantabulous help. Merry Christmas, everyone!— M.C.

For my mum, Judy, who has always loved Christmas.— D.M.

Danielle McDonald

Scholastic Australia
An imprint of Scholastic Australia Pty Limited
PO Box 579 Gosford NSW 2250
ABN 11 000 614 577
www.scholastic.com.au

Part of the Scholastic Group
Sydney • Auckland • New York • Toronto • London • Mexico City • New Delhi • Hong Kong • Buenos Aires • Puerto Rico

Published by Scholastic Australia in 2020.

NATIONAL LIBRARY OF AUSTRALIA

A catalogue record for this book is available from the National Library of Australia

ISBN: 978-93-5471-512-9

Typeset in Sweetie Pie.

This reprint edition September 2025

Printed in India at Shivam Offset Press, New Delhi

ELLA Diaries

Christmas Crackers

Friday afternoon

Dear Diary,

It is (almost) the end of the year!

All my friends at school are buzzing around like buzzy Christmas beetles, talking about importerant things like:

1 Where they are going this year for the Christmas holidays, and

2a what they would really, really, REALLY like for Christmas, and

2b what they will probably ~~acksh~~ actually get instead, and

3 all the yummy Christmas treats and snacks they are going to make. (And also eat.)

Even our excellent (and exceptionally stylish) teacher Ms Weiss is buzzing!

And guess what she told our class today!

We're all going to be doing a special class Christmas project! From now until the very lasterest last day of the school year!*

* Well, not the absolutely lasterest last one. That's the day we have a special assembly that Mr Martini and Mrs Sneed and all the other importerant old people who work at our school but aren't ~~acksh~~ actually teachers come to. And they give long B-O-R-I-N-G with a capital B speeches about what a good year it's been and how proud they are of all our ~~acheev~~ achievements.

And then after that we go back to our classrooms and do **Secret Santa** present-giving, and eat Christmassy snacks and play Christmas-themed party games like **Pin the Tail on the Reindeer**. (Not all at the same time. That would just be weird.)

Anyway, as soon as Ms Weiss told us about doing a special project, Fiona McTavish's arm shot up high into the air. As high as the **shining star** on the very toppest part of a Christmas tree.

'Yes, Fiona,' said Ms Weiss.

So then Fiona asked Ms Weiss what the special project was going to be.

And guess what? Ms Weiss wants US to come up with our own ideas for it. And the besterest one that everyone likes the most will be the one we do!

Zoe and I looked at each other with shiny eyes. So shiny we could see Ms Weiss's sparkly Christmas tree earrings reflected in them.

Zoe and I **ALWAYS** have fantabulously fabulous ideas for projects. It is one of our **SECRET POWERS**.

Another **secret power** we have is that we can (mostly) read each other's minds! So we both know what we are thinking about inside our brain parts, even before we say it!*

* This is one of the reasons why we are

BFFFEs.**

** BFFFE means Best Friends Forever For Ever.

Here are some of the ideas that people in our class came up with. Ms Weiss wrote each one on the whiteboard so we could vote on them later.

1 Peter and Raf and George

Build a giant waterslide in the playground and take turns sliding down it into a pool of muddy mud at the bottom. (Eww.)

2 Princess Peach Parker and her handmaidens Prinny and Jade

Set up a TV studio in our classroom and do a Breakfast Show (only at lunchtime) and invite REAL celebrities to be interviewed on it by Peach.

③ Fiona McTavish

Teach everyone how to do Highland Dancing and have some Scottish Highland Games, with bagpipering and caber-tossing.

4 Georgia and Chloe and Poppy and Daisy

Knit pazillions of teeny tiny woolly jumpers for little penguins whose feathers have been trapped in sticky oil dumped from big ships. The jumpers will help keep them warm and also stop them from licking all the poisonous oil off their feathers.

THIS ONE was a GOOD one, almost as GOOD as OURS.

FINALLY (after a whole lot of extremely boring ideas) it was **OUR** turn.

I was just opening my mouth to tell Ms Weiss all about our excellent idea when

Sorry, Diary, I have to stop writing now. Olivia just banged on the door and told me Dad wants me to help him with dinner.

STRAIGHTAWAY RIGHT NOW IMMEDIATELY.

I will tell you more after dinner, I promise!

Yours forever,
Ella
XOXO

Friday night, after dinner

Dearest Diary,

Here is Zoe's and my excellent project idea.

We could do a play! With Christmas themes! Because it's nearly Christmas!

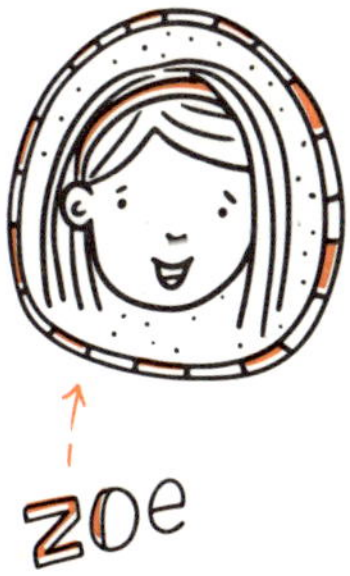

A play is PERFECT for ~~me~~ us.

That's because there would be something for EVERYONE in our class to do.

Like actoring

and dancing

and directoring the dancers and actors so they know what to do.

And there
can be music
played on
real musical
instruments
by real
musicians

and sweet little costumes designed by ~~me~~
a head costume designerer

and handpainted sets for everyone in the play to walk around in front of, so the people watching the play know where it is happening.

It would be aMAZing. And Excellent. And fanTABulously fabulous!

And guess what? Our idea got the most votes! Out of all the ideas!

Which means LOTS of people must have liked it. Even Precious Princess Peach Parker!* Peach NEVER usually likes any of the ideas I suggest.

* Probably because she wants to be one of the main play people. Like the main actorer. Or the number one dancer. Or the head designerer. Or . . .

Da da da . . . dummmm!

Maybe even the directorer!

NOOOOOOOOOooo!

And guess what else? Ms Weiss said we are going to start doing all the stuff you need to do when you are doing a play **FIRST THING** on Monday morning!

Which means we only have the weekend to think up all the ideas for it! And there's just **SO MUCH TO DO!** So we asked our other friend Ammy if she wanted to be on our End of Year Class Play Committee (EOYCPC). Ammy **ALWAYS** has excellent ideas for things like that too.

And guess what she said?

Do you want to Be ON OUR PLAY COMMITTEE?
It's going to Be FUNNEROUS FUN!
NO.
????!!!
PHEW.
ONLY Joking! of course I DO!
Ha Ha!

Hehehe. Ammy is SOOO FUNNY sometimes. ☺

The first thing we need to do is have an EPCM (Emergency Play Committee Meeting) here at my house, so we can discuss all the importerant things we need to do about the play.

I'm going to ask Mum about it tomorrow morning, as soon as I wake up.

I CAN'T WAIT!

Love,
Ella

Saturday morning

Dear Diary,

I am in desperating despair. ☹

I just asked Mum about Zoe and Ammy coming here for our EPCM. And she said, 'Sorry, darling. We are going to be very busy ALL DAY. How about tomorrow instead?'

She wouldn't even change her mind, even though I used all my special Powers of Persuasion (POPs).

So instead of settling down in my comfy bedroom for a nice relaxing Emergency Meeting with my two best friends, I had to go with Mum to a **fancy** hairdressing salon at the shopping mall. So Olivia and Max could get haircuts.

It's **SO NOT FAIR**, Diary. Olivia and Max didn't even *need* haircuts. Well, OK, maybe a *bit*.

And we couldn't do our EPCM *after* lunch because we all had to go to Golden Gardens to visit my Great-nanna Peggy for her end-of-year concert.

All the Golden Oldies were doing a singalong of ancient songs in exTREMEly louderous voices.

And then after that there was a fabulous afternoon tea, with lots of food that Golden Oldies love to eat. Like scones and jam and cream, and sweet little fairy cakes.

So by the time we got home there was NO TIME AT ALL LEFT for our EPCM. Not even ten minutes.

Oh well. I suppose there is always tomorrow.

Good night, Diary.

Speak again soon (I hope).

Yours,

Ella x

Sunday night

Dearest Diary,

We had our EPCM!

And it was amazing! And excellent! And fantabulously fabulous!

First of all we ate all the snacks. Zoe even brought over one of her Nonna's special chocolate cakes!

Then we set up our official End of Year Class Play Committee. And also made our badges for it.

Here are all the people on the committee and what they do.

PRESIDENT (main person in charge of everything): Ella
VICE-PRESIDENT (who gets to be president if the REAL president is sick/and or away): Zoe
TREASURER (person in charge of all the treasure)*: Ammy

* I am not totally one hundred per cent sure what a Treasurer ~~acksh~~ actually does. So I just made this part up for now.

Zoe was worried she didn't have any REAL jobs to do. So she is now also Official Person in Charge of Jotting Down Ideas as well as Vice-President.

Next Ammy told us that she really, really, REALLY wanted to be Play Directorer.

I was shocked!

It was so not fair, Diary. I'm ALWAYS talking about how much I want to be an internationally famous play directorer. Ammy and Zoe should know how importerant it is to me to do that job. ☹

Ammy and I glared at each other for a bit with VERY unshiny eyes. And then Zoe (happily) had a brilliant idea.

So Ammy and I stopped glaring at each other and had a quick game of Rock, Paper, Scissors instead. (Phew.)

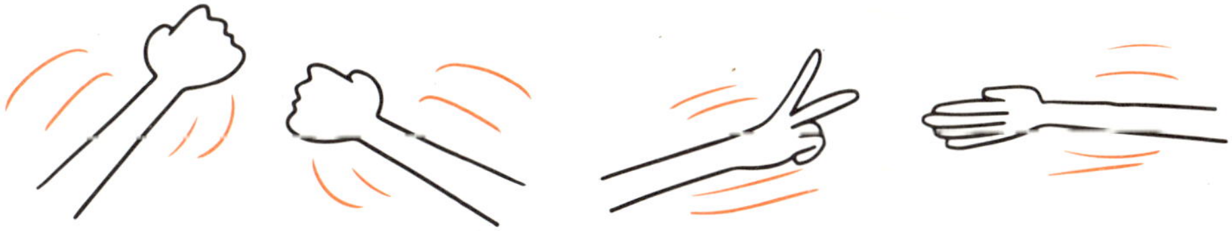

And guess who won?

HINT: The answer rhymes with what Golden Oldies like to drink!

☺☺☺

So now I'm the Head Directorer of Plays. Ammy is very good at organising things, so she's going to be Head Stage Manager. She gets to tell everyone where to stand and make sure they are wearing the right costume and other importerant stuff like that.

And Zoe is **exTREMEly** artistical. So she's going to be Head Set Designerer, in charge of all the set painterers.

~~Unforch~~ Unfortunately we used up our **WHOLE MEETING TIME** ~~arguing about~~ discussing who was going to do which job. Which means we didn't get **ANY TIME AT ALL** to ~~ac.k.sh~~ actually write our play. Or even decide what it is going to be about.

And our class project starts tomorrow! First thing!

OOPS!

Ella

X

Monday, after school

Dear Diarydoo,

Something really aMAZing happened when Zoe and Ammy and I were walking to school this morning.

Here's what we all said.

Ammy (worried): We are going to be in SO much trouble from Ms Weiss.

Zoe (more worried): I know.

Me (even more worried): I can't believe we haven't even written our play yet. When we had the WHOLE WEEKEND to do it!

Zoe: I know. Did you have any good ideas for it last night, Ammy?

Ammy: Nope.

Zoe: Me neither. ☹

Ammy: Maybe we could do something about Christmas?

We all stared off into space for a bit, imagining all the exciting Christmassy things that would be fun to do in a play.

And then I suddenly had the most aMAZingly Excellent idea.

Me (excitedly): I know! Last year Nanna Kate took us to see this fantabulous play! And it was all about Christmas! (Mostly.) No, wait—it was a ballet. With lots of dancing.

Zoe: Yes! I love dancing!

Ammy: What was it called?

Me: I can't remember. But there was a giant nutcracker in it.

Ammy: Is that like a Christmas cracker that two people pull the ends of until it goes POP? And then party hats and little jokes fall out and you have to read them?

Me: Nope. It's a wooden thing you use to crack nuts open. I think the one in the play looked like a toy soldier.

Zoe: So was there a giant nut too? To go in the giant nutcracker?

Me: Probably. And also a girl. Two girls maybe? And lots of snowy snow. And swirling snowflakes. And they went to lots of different lands.

Ammy: What kind of lands?

Me: I think one of them was called the Land of Chickens.

Zoe: We could go there in our play too. And do a Chicken Dance!

Me: Yes! That is perfect! Zoe, you are aMAZing!

Zoe: ☺☺☺

Me: You too, Ammy.

Ammy: ☺☺☺☺☺☺

We finally had a play! ☺

As soon as school started properly, Zoe and Ammy and I raced up to Ms Weiss's desk and told her all our exciting plans for it.

Me (enthusiastically): We've got our play idea all worked out! It's going to be aMAZing!

Zoe (also enthusiastically): It's all about Christmas! And there's going to be a giant nutcracker!

Ammy (even more enthusiastically): And a giant nut!

Ms Weiss (super impressed): Good work, girls. I can't wait to read it!

Me, Zoe and Ammy (together): ☺☺☺

Zoe: I'm going to design all the sets for it. And Ammy's going to be Head Stage Manager.

Me: And I'm going to to be the Head Directorer. And also the Head Costume Designerer. And the Person in Charge of **EVERYTHING!**

Ms Weiss (overwhelmed): Ummm . . . well . . .

And then Ms Weiss told us (kindly) that maybe doing **ALL** of those things might be a little bit too much for just three people. Even three people as talented and wonderfully organised as us. EsPECially as we only had a few days to do **THE WHOLE PLAY** and everything in it! (OOPS!)

So now Ms Weiss is going to be the Head Directorer. And she's going to ask some of the other teachers (like our art and craft teacher Ms Kahlo, and Mr Zugaro, my old teacher from last year) to help out with the costumes and sets as well.

Zoe and Ammy and I were **SHOCKED!**

And also sad. We'd spent **HOURS** making our EOYCPC badges. And now we weren't even going to get to wear them. ☹

But then Ms Weiss told us she still wanted us to write the play. And that it sounded aMAZing! Especially the part about the giant nut. So that cheered us all up a bit. ☺

And we could go to the library to work on it **STRAIGHTAWAY RIGHT THEN**, while everyone else had to just stay behind doing boring, ordinary, normal work.

So we did.

First we worked out all the names of our characters.

Here are the four main ones.

And then **all the things** that are going to happen to them.

And also the dance we are going to do.

And then after recess we reported back to our class about our play.

Everyone was **amazed!** And also **excitered**. Even Princess Peach. (Again!)

It was really weird, Diary.

She kept giving me these really big smiles (that showed off all her sharkerous shark teeth).

I can't wait until tomorrow when we start rehearsing our play!

Love,
Ella
XOXO

Tuesday, after school

Dearest Diary,

We had our first proper play meeting with the whole class today.

Zoe and Ammy and I sat out the front, wearing our new, improved badges.

First of all Ms Weiss asked everyone else what they wanted to do. These were the **four groups** they could choose from.

ACTORING

DANCING

SET PAINTING AND PROP* FINDERERS

REAL LIVE MUSIC-PLAYING

* Prop is the special actoring name for the things you have on stage when you are doing a play. Like a giganterous (fake) Christmas cake or a toy chicken.

Most people wanted to do actoring, so that was the biggest group.

But hardly ANYONE wanted to do live music-playing. Only Lila, who plays the drums. And also Fiona McTavish.

So Ms Weiss decided we should use RECORDED music that you play through speakers instead.

Then Ammy did a little speech where she told everyone all the things that are going to happen in the play. And also the names of all the main characters.

And guess what? Everyone clapped at the end! Especially Ms Weiss.

Although I think she must have an extremely bad cold at the moment, because she kept covering her mouth with her hand and scrunching up her eyes while Ammy was talking.

Like the part where villainous villain Norman Nutcracker is trying to catch Neddy the Giant Nut so he can crack him open and eat him*.

* ~~Forch~~ Fortunately for Neddy, he has a **secret power** which means he can **NEVER** be cracked open.

Not even if you tried for a pazillion bazillion years in a row.

And also the part where Vernice (who is exceptionally braverous and talented) and her BFF Tia are in their sleigh, also trying to run away from villainous Norman.

And then they travel through a magical portal into the Land of Chickens.

After Ammy finished all her explaining and describing, Ms Weiss pinned some lists up on the back wall so the actoring people could write their names against the parts they wanted to play.

I was **secretly hoping** that nobody would write their name down next to Vernice, the main girl in the play.

And then I would just (casually) say something to Zoe and Ammy like. 'Ooooo, look. No-one wants to be Vernice. Now what are we going to do?'

And then I could (equally casually) offer to play her role (as well as being Head Play writer).

But tragically, all my secret hopes were IN ~~VEIN~~ VAIN, dear Diary. That is because pazillions of people DID write their names next to Vernice on the page. So many names that there wasn't enough room for them all to fit, and the last ones were squasherated up against each other.

Like this.

ACTOR PARTS
VERNICE
Georgia
Jessie
Ammy
Peach
Jade
Fiona
poppy
Zoe
Prinny
Chloe
Daisy
Ella
TIA
NORMAN NUTCRACKER
RAF
NEDDY THE GIANT NUT
George

Then Chloe asked if there would need to be tryouts for the part of Vernice now.

I was just about to answer **yes**, when Ms Weiss explained that, sadly, there wasn't enough time.

And then Ms Weiss said, 'Any one of you would make a wonderful Vernice.'

She told us that we should just put all the names in a hat and draw out **a winner**. And then draw out a **SECOND** name to be Tia, Vernice's BFF. (Because nobody had put their name next to that part.)

So we did. And guess who the winner was?

If you said Chloe or Georgia or Poppy or Daisy or Fiona or Jessie (or me) you are wrong, wrong, **WRONG!**

WARNING: Tissue alert

It was Peach. Precious Perfect Princess Peach Parker.

How does she do it, Diary? How does Princess Peach always get **EVERYTHING SHE WANTS, EVERY SINGLE TIME?**

It is **SO** not fair. ☹☹☹

So then Ms Weiss pulled a second name out of the hat, and this time it was Chloe.

But then Chloe said she'd changed her mind about doing actoring and could she be a dancing chicken instead. And so did Georgia and Poppy and Daisy.

And then both Prinny and Jade asked if they could be Tia at EXACTLY the same time. Like this.

And then Prinny and Jade had a big ~~fight~~ argument about it because they both wanted to be Vernice's BFF Tia in the play really, REALLY badly. (Almost as badly as Ammy and I both wanted to be Head Directorer.)

It was all so DRAMATIC, Diary. And we weren't even doing the play yet!

Everyone else looked **SHOCKED!**

So then Ms Weiss (quietly) asked me if maybe the play could be changed so that Vernice would have **TWO** best friends, instead of only one.

I was just about to ask Ms Weiss if we could have an emergency Play Writing Committee Meeting so we could talk about this when—

DOOT!

DOOT!

DOOT!

The bell went.

And Ms Weiss said she needed to have an answer for the best friends problem **straightaway right now**.

So I just said yes instead.

So now Vernice has two BFFs. Tia and Mia.

Putting on a play is very hard work, Diary! ☹

I have to stop writing now because Zoe and Ammy are coming over to my house in EXACTLY FIVE MINUTES and I need to get ready for them.

Only this time we're not having a play committee meeting. We're going to be doing something COMPLETELY DIFFERENT.

But I can't tell you what it is yet. It's a SECRET. ☺

CU Tomorrow.

Love,

Ella

XOXO

Wednesday, after school

Dear Diary,

We had a rest from all the play drama today because it was a BUDDY DAY! ☺

On their very first day of school, all the little new kids get matched up with a grown-up Grade 5 buddy (like me). And then all the buddies get to hang out with them for a few hours every few weeks.

It's fun!

My buddy is called Isobel and she is **sooo cute**. And so are Inez and Samilla—Zoe and Ammy's buddies. We all hang out together on Buddy Days and do amazing and excellent stuff, like making up stories about naughty princesses and good dragons, or playing shops with pinecones under the big trees.

But today we did something really different. We took them on a Treasure Hunt!

Hehehe. Making the Treasure Hunt is the **secret thing** that Zoe and Ammy and I were doing last night.

First we made a list of all the places our buddies had to go to on the way to finding their treasure.

Our buddies aren't very good at reading complicated things like clues yet. So we **drew all the places** on a giganterous Treasure Map.

Like this.

And then today we used our Buddy Time to help them find all the places on the map.

IT WAS FUNNEROUS FUN!

Especially when they found their treasure. ☺

Isobel gave me a **big squishy hug** to say thank you. And Inez and Samilla gave Zoe and Ammy big hugs as well.

Then they did a little happy dance, just for us.

Zoe and I gave each other a big look. And then we both said **EXACTLY** the same thing at **EXACTLY** the same time.

Like this.

And then we did it again!

Zow-ie. It must be the secret mind-reading power in our brain parts again!

Ammy thought it was an excellent idea as well. So we asked our buddies if they would like to do a special dance in our play. With sweet little outfits on.

And guess what they said!

It's going to be aMAZing! And FABULOUS! And FUNnerous FUN!

Love,
Ella
x

Thursday night, in bed

Dear Diary,

We did more work on our play today! Ammy and I went to the library to write our script, which is the special actoring word for what everyone says in the play.

We kept all the talking parts super short to make it easy for all the actorers to remember them. ☺

Mr Snarski helped us a bit.

Zoe and all the other artistical kids went to **the art room**, so Ms Kahlo could help them to paint the sets.

And also make a sleigh for the reindeer to ~~hort~~ ~~hawt~~ haul across the stage.

Except it's not going to be a REAL sleigh. That would just be weird. (And also exTREMEly trickerous to make. How would we even find all the parts for it? EsPECially the reindeer.)

So we're just going to make one side of the sleigh, out of cardboard. And then Vernice and her besties Tia and Mia are going to pretend to be sitting in it. (When they are really just walking behind it.)

Like this.

And Lila and Fiona are going to dress up as reindeer and pretend to be hauling the sleigh across the stage.

Chloe and Georgia and Poppy and Daisy started working out the steps for their **Chicken Dance** in the big hall with Ms Astrellano.

And everyone else stayed in our classroom, making pazillions of teeny tiny snowflakes with Ms Weiss.

And guess what? Ms Weiss ~~loves~~ ADORES our idea of getting ALL the buddies to do a dance. She thinks it will be really sweet. And also a lovely way for everyone to finish off their Buddy year.

Now all we have to do is work out a dance for them to do!

And also teach it to them.

That's going to be EASY-PEASY for sure. ☺

Bye for now,
Love,
Ella

About ten minutes later . . .

I just had the most excellentest idea I have ever had IN MY WHOLE LIFE!

The buddies can do a snowflake dance!

Right before the part in the play where Vernice and Tia and Mia are in their sleigh and get hauled across the stage by the reindeer! To show that they are in an eXTREMEly snowy place!

And they can dress up in sweet little snowflake outfits with snow-white leotards, tutus, or leggings. And also furry ears and mittens to keep their teeny tiny hands warm. Like this.

Ella ☺

About ten minutes after that . . .

I just had *another* Excellent idea!

We can get some other people from our grade (like Cordelia and some of the other prop-findering ones) to throw handfuls of the snowflakes our class is busily making all over the buddies. **While they are dancing!!**

with **GIGANTEROUS FANS** on the side of the stage to blow them around and around!

So it looks like the paper snowflakes are swirling around in the sky and then landing on the buddy snowflakes!

And we could glitterise the paper ones first to make them all sparkly and shiny and glittery!

It is going to look aMAZing! And also exCEPtionally DRAMATIC! Just like a REAL play!

I can't wait until tomorrow to tell Zoe and Ammy ALL about it!

Ella ☺

Friday night, in bed

Dear Diary,

Zoe and Ammy and I had an EPCM as soon as we got to school so I could tell them all about my buddy snowflake dancing idea. And also the glitterised snowflake throwing.

And they thought both my ideas were excellent! Especially the glitterising part.

And so did Ms Weiss and Mrs Finkel, the main person in charge of Buddy Days.

So we are now officially adding the **Buddy Snowflake Dance** to the play! ☺

The first thing we did was work out some dance steps for the buddies to do. This was easy-peasy for Zoe and me, because of all the years and years and YEARS we learned proper dancing at La Madame Fry École du Ballet*.

* Which is just the fancy way of saying Mrs Fry's Ballet School. In French.

We decided they could do some toe-pointering

and arm-twinkling

and twisting from side to side

and little hops and jumps.

We asked all the other kids in our class to bring their buddies—and also our three-over to the big hall.

Then we showed them all the different steps. Mrs Finkel and the big buddies helped the little buddies when they couldn't remember what to do.

Hehehe. Peter and Raf were *really* funny.

Inez and Samilla were *really* good at dancing. They pointed their teensy tiny toes and twinkled their arms in all the right places.

And guess what? They go to Mrs Fry's Ballet School too! They're in the junior class, with all the other little kids.

Isobel doesn't go with them, though. She couldn't remember ANY of the steps we showed her. Not even one. And when we tried to show her how to do toe-pointering, she sat down on the floor with her back to everybody. Like this.

I hope she remembers how to do her steps by the time of our BIG PERFORMANCE next week . . .

Love,

Ella

XOXO

Saturday night

Dear Diary,

You will never ever guess what happened today!

Mum and Dad said they had to go on an URGENT MISSION to do some super-secret Christmas business. They wouldn't tell us what the secret business was, even though we asked them a pazillion bazillion times*.

* I bet I know what they were doing though . . . Present buying! Hehehe. ☺

So Nanna Kate took Olivia and Max and me on a lovely trip to The Secret Garden Café while they were gone. The café is in the Community Gardens, where Nanna Kate does lots of weeding and checking her plants for snails with other ancient people. (Snails. Eww.)

And guess who was there?

You never will so I'll just tell you.

My buddy, Isobel! And her Nanna Sheena!

Nanna Kate and Nanna Sheena are gardening buddies. Which is almost the same as Isobel and me!

Nanna Kate asked Isobel's nanna to sit with us, but she said they were just leaving.

So I gave Isobel a big smile and she gave me a teensy tiny little one back. Then she gave me a big hug.

Like this. ☺

After they left I told Nanna Kate all about our snowflake dance for the play, and how Isobel was having trouble remembering all the steps.

Hmmm. Maybe they're right. I'm going to have to think up a new plan to help her out . . .

Love,

Ella

Sunday night

Dear Diary,

Zoe and Ammy and I had our last, final play meeting today. That's because our Christmas play is going to be on in only TWO MORE SLEEPS!

Everyone in the WHOLE SCHOOL is going to be there. And maybe even some mums and dads and nannas and grandads as well.

First we cut out some more snowflakes, and glitterised them.

Then we borrowed the big fan from Mum's study so we could practise swirling them around the room.

~~Unforch~~ Unfortunately, we made a bit of a mess.

OOPS!

Hopefully everything will be **alright on the night!**

Wish us luck, Diary!

Yours 4 ever and ever,

Ella

Monday, after school

Dear Diary,

Today was a SUPER importerant and busy day. SO busy I thought my head was going to explode.

SCALE OF BUSY-NESS

We had the dress rehearsal for our play. And there were BAZILLIONS of importerant things to do. Like:

1. Making sure all the actors were saying all the right words from the script.

2. Checking to see that the set painterers were painting the right backdrop.

3. Practising the Snowflake Dance WITHOUT the Chicken Dancers getting in the way.

4. Giving my buddy Isobel a secret private Snowflake Dance lesson until she knew all the steps in the right order PERFECTLY OFF BY HEART.

5 Finding a special sparkly tiara at the VERY LAST MINUTE because Princess Peach insisted on being a real princess* in the play and said if she didn't get one straightaway she was going to Q-U-I-T with a capital Q.

*Which meant I also had to change her name in the script from plain old Vernice to *Princess* Vernice. ☹

6 Organising an emergency meeting because we'd totally forgotten to think up a name for our play. OOPS!

Everybody LOVED that idea. ☺☺☺☺☺

Being Head Play Writer and Person in Charge of Snowflake Dancering is exTREMEly HARD WORK, Diary.

I am going to stop writing now so I can have a nice relaxing sleep.

Good night
Sleep tight
Don't let
The naughty Giant Nutcracker
Bite.
(Or crack you open and eat you!)

Ella ☺

Tuesday night, very late

Dear Diary,

We did our play!

The Good News

Everyone loved it!

And they did lots of laughing! (Even in the **TRAGICAL** and **DEEPLY DRAMATIC** parts where it wasn't supposed to be funny.)

The Bad News

George (who was playing the part of the giant nut) got all tangled up in his nut costume and couldn't see properly.
So he kept wobbling around the stage and bumping into people.

And also into the props.

And then he almost **fell off the stage!**

~~Forch~~ Fortunately Zoe ran over and stopped him just in time.

PHEW!

After that it was time for Princess Vernice and Tia and Mia to set off in their sleigh through the snowy snow. Which meant it was time for our Buddy Swirling Snowflake dance! .

YES!!!!!!

Except . . .

Da Da Da... DUMMMmm.

Two of the buddy snowflakes said they didn't want to be in the play anymore, right at the very lasterest last moment. ☹

And then they started crying, really louderously, so that everyone could hear them.

Cordelia ran over and gave them Mr Wombat and his friend Miss Meerkat for a quick cuddle.

And then their big buddies jumped up onto the stage with them and held their hands throughout the WHOLE ENTIRE swirling snowflake dance. Like this.

And guess what else? Two of the buddies got bored of doing toe-pointering and arm twinkling.

So they made up their own snowflake dance instead. It was aMAZing!

Our next big scene was the one where Vernice and Mia and Tia's sleigh gets hauled across the stage until it reaches the **magical portal** that will take them into the Land of Chickens.

Ammy came out from the side of the stage (dressed all in black so nobody could see her) and held up a hula hoop.

Then, one by one, Vernice and Mia and Tia (and also the reindeer) climbed through it.

Except, sadly, the last reindeer got one of her antlers stuck.

So Ammy and Ms Kahlo (who was dressed up as a Christmas Cracker) had to give her a bit of a push to get her through.

Finally it was time for the Chicken Dance. And you'll **NEVER** guess what happened. Lila brought along some **REAL LIVE** chickens in a cat carrier to go with it!

FOXY SOXY ROXY

She carefully opened up the little gate on the carrier. Foxy, Soxy and Roxy stuck their heads out and had a quick look around.

Then they strutted out and started wandering around the stage, pecking at the floorboards.

'SQUAWK!' said Foxy. Then she did a big poo right in the middle of the stage.

OOPS!

Then Soxy fluttered over to Vernice's sleigh and perched right on top of it. Peach **SCREAMED!** Like this.

DOUBLE OOPS!

So then Lila ran across the stage to try to catch Roxy before she did something really naughty too—like laying an egg. Just as Chloe and Georgia and Poppy and Daisy came on to start their dance.

And the audience clapped and cheered thunderously!

CLAP! CLAP! CLAP!

It was aMAZing. And Excellent. And fanTABulously fabulous!

Love,

Ella

XOXO

PS The next day

Today was the very lasterest day of term.

And guess what Mr Martini did at our special assembly?

He gave our class a giganterous box of REAL Christmas Crackers!

Then he said our play was the BEST (and also FUNNIEST) play he'd seen in the history of plays! And he hopes that we will write and perform ANOTHER play next year!

ELLA Diaries

Read more of Ella's brilliant diary in

- Double Dare You
- Ballet Backflip
- I ♥ Pets
- Dreams Come True
- Christmas Chaos
- Pony School Showdown
- Friends Not Forever
- Worst Camp Ever
- Operation Merry Christmas
- Friendship S.O.S
- Going Green
- Total TV Drama
- Goal Power
- Diary Disaster
- The Super Secret Club
- Gym Squad Tumble
- Time to Shine
- Wildlife Rescue!
- Passion for Fashion

and look out for more coming soon!